How Can I Help?
Friends Helping Friends™

HELPING A FRIEND
WHO IS
DEPRESSED

Richard Worth

ROSEN
PUBLISHING

New York

Published in 2017 by The Rosen Publishing Group, Inc.
29 East 21st Street, New York, NY 10010

Library of Congress Cataloging-in-Publication Data

Names: Worth, Richard, 1975– author.
Title: Helping a friend who is depressed / Richard Worth.
Description: First edition. | New York : Rosen Publishing, 2017. | Series:
  How can I help? Friends helping friends | Audience: Grades 7–12. |
  Includes bibliographical references and index.
Identifiers: LCCN 2016017418| ISBN 9781499464429 (library bound) | ISBN
  9781499464405 (pbk.) | ISBN 9781499464412 (6-pack)
Subjects: LCSH: Depression, Mental—Juvenile literature. | Depression in
  adolescence—Juvenile literature.
Classification: LCC RC537 .W668 2017 | DDC 616.85/27—dc23
LC record available at https://lccn.loc.gov/2016017418

Manufactured in China

CONTENTS

INTRODUCTION

In this sad world of ours sorrow comes to all and it often comes with bitter agony. Perfect relief is not possible except with time. You cannot now believe that you will ever feel better. But this is not true. You are sure to be happy again. Knowing this, truly believing it will make you less miserable now. I have had enough experience to make this statement.

—Abraham Lincoln

Abraham Lincoln—the man who saved the Union during the Civil War—is considered one of America's greatest presidents. But while he was leading the North to victory, Lincoln was also battling serious, almost paralyzing, depression. In Lincoln's time, depression was called "melancholia," and some people who suffered extreme forms were treated in asylums.

Mark Twain, the humorous storyteller and world-famous author of *Tom Sawyer* and *Huckleberry Finn*, also suffered from depression that sent him into deep, dark moods. And Princess Diana, one of the world's most glamorous women, was also a victim of terrible depression. No matter how famous or how great or how beautiful you may be, you may suffer from major depression.

Depression is a psychological illness, or a mood disorder. The Greek physician Hippocrates first diagnosed the disorder more than two thousand years ago. He believed that

During most of his life, Abraham Lincoln suffered from serious depression, called melancholia in the 1800s.

dark humors affected the brain, causing depression. Hippocrates also became the first doctor to treat the illness with medicine and counseling. Later, during the Middle Ages, people attributed depression to God's retribution against sinners who had angered him.

During the twentieth century, psychiatrists led by Sigmund Freud recognized that depression had a psychological origin. Mental health experts also realized that depression might have a genetic cause—that is, it could be an inherited illness that was passed on from one generation to the next. Medical professionals have now developed antidepressant drugs that are used along with talk therapy to treat patients suffering from depression.

According to the National Institute of Mental Health, more than 6.5 percent of American adults suffer from major depression—more than 8 percent of women and almost 5 percent of men. The illness affects people in almost every age bracket and in every racial group, from adolescents to adults over fifty.

The National Institute of Mental Health adds that "major depression is a common mental disorder affecting adolescents in the United States." This type of depression is defined as a period "of two weeks or longer during which there is either depressed mood or loss of interest or pleasure" and other symptoms such as "problems with sleep, eating, energy, concentration, and self-image." More then 11 percent of adolescents, 15.7 million people, suffer from major depression. The illness is approximately three times more common among girls as it is among boys.

Unlike in Lincoln's day, there are now extensive resources available for those suffering from major depression. No one needs to feel alone, afraid to share their problems with someone else—whether a friend or family member or professional. As a friend, there are important things you can do to help and support someone who is suffering from depression.

CHAPTER ONE

WHAT IS MAJOR DEPRESSION?

All of us can recall situations when we felt sad or temporarily depressed. Perhaps you studied extra hard for an important test and still failed to receive a high grade. Or perhaps one of your parents got a new job and you had to move to a new city, leaving behind your closest friends. It's natural to feel unhappy about these experiences, and for a time they may seem overwhelming. But these feelings soon pass, and life's balance is restored.

This is called reactive depression. That is when a person is feeling depressed in reaction to a specific event, such as a poor test grade or a problem at home.

Major, or clinical, depression, however, is quite different. With clinical depression, negative feelings are much stronger and last far longer, affecting every aspect of an individual's life. This may leave someone completely incapable of managing his or her own day-to-day living. Clinical depression often emerges in adolescence because it is a period of so many other changes.

Your body is growing physically. You can see some of these changes in your arms and legs. But others are far less obvious, and the most important of these occur in your brain. As your brain grows, it makes new connections between important nerve cells. Meanwhile, your body is producing sex hormones that may influence the development of your brain. If these hormonal changes combine with a major change in your life, the resulting emotional stress may lead to clinical depression.

These trigger events, as they are called, can include a significant change in your life—such as your parents' divorce, the death of a beloved relative or family member, or a violent incident involving a close friend. These traumatic life events put you at greater risk for developing depression.

A "trigger event" such as the death of a close friend or a member of your family can lead to clinical depression.

Genetic history is another risk factor in depression. Perhaps one of your parents has battled depression for many years. Or one of your grandparents suffered from clinical depression. This may put you at greater risk for developing the illness.

Some adolescents also suffer from serious anxiety. Anxiety is a general feeling that something unpleasant is always about to happen. For instance, even though you regularly study hard for tests, you're continuously afraid of not doing well. Or social situations may fill you with so much anxiety that you'd rather stay home. Anxiety frequently morphs into depression. Your general fears cause you to look at life through a negative lens, as if the "glass is always half empty," never "half full."

Of course, adolescence is a period that often produces natural anxiety. Doing well in school becomes particularly important, especially if you're planning to apply to college. Friendships and peer groups are very important to help us cope with adolescence. So it's easy to become anxious about the strength of our friendships and feel anxious any time they seem to be in jeopardy.

Perhaps this is one of the reasons that girls appear more susceptible to adolescent depression than boys. In her book *American Girls: Social Media and the Secret Lives of Teenagers*, author Nancy Jo Sales explains that the teenage girls she interviewed were constantly checking social media on their cell phones to find out where they stood with their friends. "The constant seeking of likes and attention on social media," Sales writes, "seems for many girls to feel like being a contestant in a never-ending beauty pageant in which they're forever performing to please the judges."

Researchers have also discovered that girls produce less serotonin than boys. Serotonin is a chemical in the brain that helps send signals from one part of the brain to another. Low production of serotonin, which occurs more often in girls than in boys, may lead to depression. That's because the brain's forty million brain cells are directly affected by serotonin. These are brain cells that influence moods, sexual desire, sleep, and social interaction.

Although more adolescent girls than boys report suffering from depression, researchers believe that this might also be because girls are far more willing than boys to admit their feelings.

OTHER CAUSES OF DEPRESSION

Another cause of depression can be stress. While some stress may be helpful because it helps us to perform more effectively, too much stress can paralyze us and bring on depression. For example, parents may constantly emphasize high performance in class or on the athletic field, almost to the exclusion of everything. Teenagers in such situations may even feel that their parents will only love them if they have an outstanding level of achievement in school, in sports, or on national tests.

Some teenagers may also experience shame, which can lead to depression. A girl's parents may emphasize the importance of good looks or compare her appearance to that of her sister or her friends. This may cause the teen to feel ashamed of how she looks, especially in comparison to other students in her class.

Psychologists feel that a teenager's own inner turmoil or conflict may also bring on depression. Many teens may want to become more independent but feel unwilling to assert themselves. And some parents discourage their children from trying anything new, wanting their teenage children to remain dependent on them. As a result, these teens may

THE COMPLEX BRAIN

Your brain sends billions of messages to the rest of your body each second. To speed these messages on their way, the brain also produces chemicals called neurotransmitters. These include norepinephrine, dopamine, and serotonin. Messages in the brain are electrical signals that travel from one nerve cell to the next. In between is

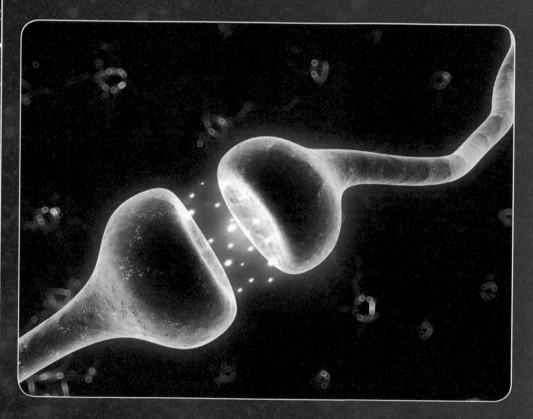

A chemical called serotonin enables messages to be transmitted across a space from one nerve cell to another. These nerve cells are successfully passing information across the synapse because they have enough serotonin.

a space called a synapse. Serotonin is released to fill that space when a signal needs to cross it. After the message is transmitted, the transmitting cell reabsorbs the serotonin. Without enough serotonin, some of the messages will not be transmitted, which can lead to feelings of depression. That's because your brain cannot effectively send messages to the rest of your body, telling it what to do and how to feel. This can affect your appetite, your sexual feelings, your ability to sleep, and your feelings of anger and self-control—all symptoms of depression.

feel depressed—torn between their desire to be like other teenagers and a need to please their parents.

SYMPTOMS OF DEPRESSION

Professor of psychiatry Stan Kutcher has developed a scale to evaluate the seriousness of depression in adolescents. The Kutcher Adolescent Depression Scale (KADS) includes eleven items, each with four possible responses: hardly ever, much of the time, most of the time, and all the time. Adolescents are asked how they would answer each question to describe their feelings over the past week.

1. Low mood, sadness, feeling blah or down, depressed, just can't be bothered.
2. Irritable, losing your temper easily.
3. Sleep difficulties—different from your usual: trouble falling asleep, lying awake in bed.

4. Feeling decreased interest in: hanging out with friends; being with your best friend; being with your boyfriend/girlfriend; going out of the house; doing schoolwork or work; doing hobbies or sports or recreation.
5. Feelings of worthlessness, hopelessness, letting people down, not being a good person.
6. Feeling tired, feeling fatigued, low in energy, hard to get motivated, have to push to get things done, want to rest or lie down a lot.
7. Trouble concentrating, can't keep your mind on schoolwork or work, daydreaming when you should be working, hard to focus when reading, getting "bored" with work or school.
8. Feeling that life is not very much fun, not feeling good when usually you would feel good, not getting as much pleasure from fun things as usual.
9. Feeling worried, nervous, panicky, tense, keyed up, anxious.
10. Physical feelings of worry like: headaches, butterflies, nausea, tingling, restlessness, diarrhea, shakes or tremors.
11. Thoughts, plans or actions about suicide or self-harm.

Depression often leaves us feeling alone, isolated, and even guilty. It's like being in a deep rut without the ability to climb out. Indeed, depression may make that rut feel even deeper.

CHAPTER TWO

DEPRESSION AND ANXIETY

Shaun was asked by his music teacher to participate in a piano recital. He selected a piece of music to perform and practiced daily, over and over, until he knew the composition by heart. On the night of the recital, with a substantial audience in attendance, Shaun decided to play first among the other students, to "get it over with," as he put it, because he was so nervous. Shaun sat down at the piano and as his fingers touched the keys, he realized that he could not remember a single note of the piece. Trying desperately to bring back his memory, Shaun finally

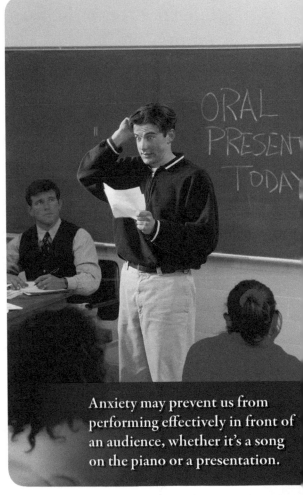

Anxiety may prevent us from performing effectively in front of an audience, whether it's a song on the piano or a presentation.

realized that it was no good. So he returned to his seat in the audience, feeling totally humiliated. His fear of failure became a self-fulfilling prophecy.

Charlotte was considered the best writer in her class. On every paper she handed in, her instructor wrote praiseworthy comments and consistently gave her an A or better. When the teacher called on Charlotte to read her papers aloud, however, she froze and began to hesitate and stutter, trying to speak the words. Indeed, Charlotte developed a stutter that began in adolescence and continued well into her adulthood. It negatively affected her relationships and undermined her success in every job.

Both Charlotte and Shaun suffered from anxiety. Generalized anxiety disorder (GAD) is a constant and uncontrollable feeling that something unexpected and unpleasant is about to happen. It seems to follow you around like a dark cloud over your head. Gerald, who suffered from GAD, confessed that he always feared that he was about to fail at his work. If the boss came into his office and closed the door, Gerald immediately thought that he was about to be fired. When his counselor asked Gerald if he had ever failed at a project or actually been fired, Gerald shook his head "no," but that didn't make the feeling go away.

Individuals suffering from GAD often experience a sick feeling in the pit of their stomach or a wooly feeling in their head as the anxiety comes on. They have a general sense of carrying around a constant burden, like a huge boulder sitting between their shoulders.

SPECIFIC DISORDERS

Sometimes, GAD attaches itself to a specific type of fear, no matter how far it may be from reality.

SOCIAL PHOBIA

This is a fear of social situations. An individual may feel anxious being in a group of other people, especially if these people are strangers. Some have fainted when confronted with this type of situation. Social phobia can be so intense that an individual feels anxiety even around friends or when making presentations in front of familiar classmates, often because the individual fears the criticism he or she might receive from others.

OBSESSIVE-COMPULSIVE DISORDER

OCD is often characterized by repetitive behavior that seems to have little or no basis in reality. Individuals may repeat certain rituals, like washing their hands over and over or going back several times to ensure that they have locked the door. Like many people with anxiety disorders, those with OCD generally lack self-confidence and suffer from low self-esteem. The repeated rituals are their way of dealing with the anxiety and trying to control it.

PANIC DISORDER

Some people with intense anxiety suffer from panic disorder, or panic attacks. The anxiety may become so overwhelming that they may not be able to leave their homes or even get out of bed. They often experience heart palpitations (a racing heart beat) and may even perspire intensely and shake. Even when an attack subsides, the individual may immediately begin to worry when another one will occur.

SEASONAL AFFECTIVE DISORDER (SAD)

Too little exposure to sunlight in winter or on rainy days in spring and summer makes some people depressed.

PHOBIAS THAT CAN AFFECT US

There are a number of irrational fears and anxieties that may afflict us. Many of these are linked to specific experiences.

Acrophobia	Fear of heights
Agoraphobia	Fear of open spaces among people
Aquaphobia	Fear of the water
Arachnophobia	Fear of spiders
Claustrophobia	Fear of small, enclosed places
Cynophobia	Fear of dogs
Trypanophobia	Fear of medical procedures involving needles

ANXIETY AND DEPRESSION

Unsurprisingly, people who suffer from severe anxiety often experience depression. That dark cloud of anxiety that they feel, waiting for something unpleasant to happen or for the next panic attack to begin, would be enough to make almost anyone feel depressed. Indeed, these two problems often accompany each other among adolescents. Researchers have discovered that approximately one-half of all young people who have clinical depression also report feeling severe

One way people can deal with SAD is by increasing the amount of artificial light they receive, a form of light therapy.

anxiety. Frequently, the anxiety precedes the depression but they may be so closely linked that it's hard to tell which came first.

Needless to say, both of these problems, or even one of them, can turn adolescence into a very unpleasant experience. If you're trying to concentrate on achieving good grades or participate on an athletic team or play a musical instrument, anxiety and depression can leave you feeling as if you're swimming through mud to reach your goals.

10 GREAT QUESTIONS TO ASK A GUIDANCE COUNSELOR

1 WHAT IS SEASONAL AFFECTIVE DISORDER (SAD)?

2 WHAT CAUSES SAD?

3 HOW IS SAD RELATED TO MAJOR DEPRESSION?

4 WHEN DOES SAD OCCUR?

5 WHAT ARE THE SYMPTOMS OF SAD?

6 HOW DOES FALL AND WINTER SAD DIFFER FROM SPRING AND SUMMER SAD?

7 HOW CAN SAD BE TREATED EFFECTIVELY?

8 WHAT IS LIGHT THERAPY?

9 HOW DOES COUNSELING HELP WITH SAD?

10 HOW DOES MEDICATION HELP WITH SAD?

CHAPTER THREE

THE FALSE ESCAPE FROM DEPRESSION

T he flight-or-fight response is among the most basic instincts in human beings. When threatened, we either decide to battle against the threat or to escape from it. Most of us have the same response to depression.

Bacchus, the Roman god of wine, was popular among people in the ancient world who tried to forget their troubles by drinking alcohol.

For centuries, people have tried to escape their problems with alcohol. The Mediterranean climate was so perfect for growing grapes that the ancient Romans could use them to make barrels and barrels of wine. One of their gods, Bacchus, was known as the god of wine, and bacchanals were drunken parties where Romans gathered to enjoy themselves and forget their troubles.

Alcohol acts as a depressant on the central nervous system. That is, it lowers brain activity, which may help a person forget what's troubling him, at least temporarily, including his depression. After the effects have worn off, however, the feelings of depression return, often accompanied by a severe headache and a queasy stomach, especially if too much alcohol has been drunk.

According to the Centers for Disease Control and Prevention, approximately 35 percent of high school students reported that they drink alcohol. More than 20 percent engage in binge drinking—consuming drink after drink until they become drunk. And about the same number admitted to riding in a car with someone who had been drinking.

Some people may take illegal drugs to help them forget their troubled feelings, or they may combine alcohol with drugs. These drugs may include substances such as marijuana, crack cocaine, ecstasy, and even prescription medications. Unfortunately, these substances often produce similar symptoms to depression. Someone on drugs may have trouble sleeping, experience severe mood swings, and lose concentration very easily. When the drugs wear off, the depression is still there. What's even worse, an individual may begin to grow dependent on drugs and keep taking them.

As a result, a depressed teenager may develop a dual diagnosis. He or she may feel depressed and also abuse drugs or alcohol. Each problem simply reinforces the other, making the depression even more severe. And this simply makes the work of dealing with depression even harder.

CUTTING AND SELF-MUTILATION

Alyssa had become seriously depressed because of what was occurring with her family. Her parents fought continually and seemed unable to agree on any issue. Her mother criticized her father for spending too much time at work and not participating in raising their children—Alyssa and her brother, Marcus. And her father criticized her mother for staying at home and not going out to work, making the family entirely dependent on his income. To cope with her own unhappiness, Alyssa's mother took more and more antidepressants, prescribed by her doctor.

Alyssa escaped by spending every evening after school in front of her computer. Unknown to her parents, she was chatting with other teenagers who were experiencing similar problems. But instead of helping each other overcome their problems, they formed a group that tried to escape by cutting themselves. Alyssa was one of them, cutting herself with a razor on her arms and legs, and then covering up the marks with her clothing.

Researchers at New Mexico State University explain that among troubled teens, "cutting is the most common method of self-injury and is often done repeatedly—it is not just a one-time occurrence." Young people use instruments such as razors, knives, glass, and even sharp stones. They may also engage in other types of self-mutilation such as biting themselves, burning their skin, or repeated deep scratching.

Why do young people like Alyssa try to escape one form of pain by inflicting another on themselves? New Mexico State scientists have found that teens may be trying "to escape from feelings of being trapped in an intolerable psychological and emotional situation in which they feel powerless. For these individuals, cutting provides temporary relief from anxiety

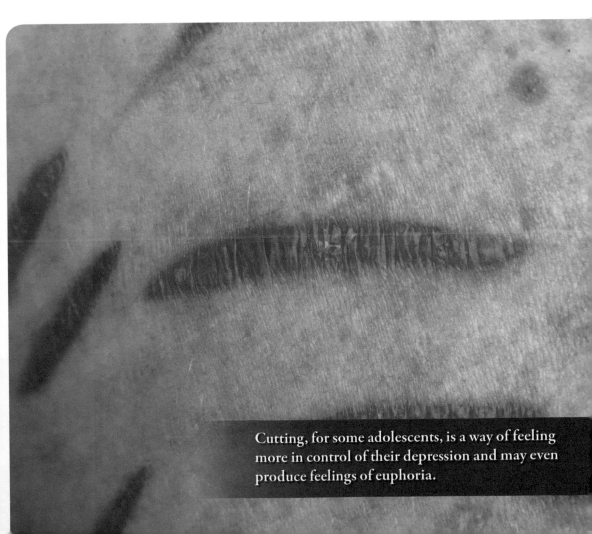

Cutting, for some adolescents, is a way of feeling more in control of their depression and may even produce feelings of euphoria.

and agitation, or provides relief from negative feelings." This may also be followed by a sense of relief after the cutting stops—much like the feelings that occur when someone stops hitting his or her head against a wall.

Cutting may also become addictive. Chemicals called endorphins are released when cutting, which may provide a teenager with a feeling of euphoria. In addition, if a teenager who is cutting herself connects with others doing the same thing, it simply reinforces the behavior.

According to the Adolescent Self Injury Foundation, approximately two million Americans engage in self-injury. These individuals cut or mutilate themselves in other ways to express their inner frustration or anger because they cannot seem to verbalize it. While experts used to believe that more females than males cut themselves, more recent research indicates that the numbers may be about the same.

CHARACTERISTICS OF PEOPLE ENGAGED IN SELF-CUTTING

- Activity begins during adolescence
- Abuse of alcohol and/or drugs
- Wearing heavy clothing during warm, summer conditions
- Spending much time alone
- Cutting devices in an adolescent's room
- Presence of blood on a teenager's clothing

EATING DISORDERS AND DEPRESSION

Some young people develop eating disorders, such as anorexia and bulimia, trying to escape their depression. Anorexia is an abnormal fear of gaining weight that leads to inadequate eating patterns, while bulimia is purging (vomiting) after eating to prevent weight gain. Eating disorders are far more common among girls, who seem to be impacted more profoundly by society's standards of attractiveness. Many women who model clothing are extremely thin, almost waif-like, and may starve themselves to maintain their weight. Teenagers who follow these role models often have an unrealistic sense of what they themselves look like or of what is a normal, healthy weight.

Anorexia and bulimia are eating disorders among teenagers who have an unhealthy self-image and may hope to control their depression by controlling their weight. Many people suffering from these disorders see themselves as fat when they are actually very thin.

Among teenagers who are also depressed, anorexia provides them with the feeling of control—they can control how much and what they eat, even when they feel unable to control their depression. Like depression, anorexia may be brought on by a traumatic event in an adolescent's life,

27

unusual levels of stress, or a significant change, such as moving to a different community and losing a circle of friends. Bulimia has similar causes.

Young people who suffer from these disorders often wear bulky clothes to disguise just how dangerously thin they have become. These eating disorders can lead to severe dehydration because young people are not getting enough fluids into their bodies. Teens may also experience lower blood pressure, accompanied by dizziness, weak muscles and bones, hair loss, and reduced brain activity.

Instead of suffering only from depression, these adolescents develop a dual diagnosis—depression and an eating disorder. Unfortunately, as time goes on and the problems persist, they become far more difficult to solve.

CHAPTER FOUR

MOMENTS OF CHANGE AND IMPROVEMENT

Being in the moment means being present in what is currently happening around you and to you. It includes enjoying the beauty of nature as you walk through a wood or a park, experiencing the diversity of other people as you encounter them, and feeling good

By reaching out to someone who appears to be suffering from constant depression and anxiety, you can help promote change and improvement.

about yourself. For many of us, especially if we suffer from chronic depression, this is extremely difficult. Often we are bound by feelings of failure and guilt from past events while suffering from anxiety about what we fear might happen in the future.

OFFERING A HELPING HAND

How do you start helping a friend who may be suffering from serious depression? Don't ignore the possible danger signs. There are often clear signals that something is wrong, even if your friend is not fully aware of it. Many young people don't recognize the signs of depression. They may think that their depressive feelings are temporary or they may not connect the feelings with some significant event in their lives.

What's more, they may not want you to know that anything is really wrong, even if you ask. They may say something like, "Oh I'm fine. Don't worry about me. I'll be OK." If you stop there, it won't help very much. So you need to prepare a follow-up: "You don't seem yourself lately. You seem tired all the time," or "You're not eating much," or "We don't spend much time together anymore."

Then you have to be willing to wait for your friend to answer. If it doesn't happen the first time that you bring up the subject, wait for another opportunity at another time. If you press too much, your friend may back away. Depression tends to isolate people, and they may not be willing to share their feelings immediately. It is important not to push your friend away by pressing too hard. Let your friend know that you support him or her regardless.

Wait for another occasion and gently raise the issue again. Don't overdo it. And if your friend doesn't immediately respond, be prepared to let silence come between you. Letting the silence build up may prompt your friend to say something. Silence can be far more powerful than anything you might say.

THE ART OF LISTENING

We live in a world of constant messaging. Big screen televisions seem to be everywhere, displaying intrusive information designed to immediately grab our attention; social media like Facebook enable us to communicate almost as soon as we think of something; and texting lets us keep those messages short, if not always meaningful.

But how many of us spend much time listening to someone else? Sharing even a few of the terrible feelings—guilt, fear, anxiety—that are all tangled up in depression may help your friend start to feel better. But this only works if someone is really and sincerely listening. Just listening, without saying very much except a few words of understanding, is often enough.

Depression can leave the people who suffer from it feeling confused. They don't really understand what is causing their depression or how to dig themselves out. But you, as a friend, can help them see a light at the end of the tunnel. You can help point the way for them with a few questions and a sincere desire to listen to their answers. This can be indispensable.

For some young people, depression may be triggered by change. Most of us can empathize with those feelings—

When doctors try to diagnose a patient's illness, they ask a series of questions to obtain important information that may relate to the problem—whether physical or psychological.

like having the rug pulled out from under us. Perhaps your family has experienced the death of a loved one—a relative, a close friend, even a beloved dog or cat. The change may be traumatic, at least for a little while, and leave you feeling depressed.

Your friend's depression may have been caused by a change in his or her life. And you might be able to help by asking if there has been any change that might have initiated your friend's feelings. This could be a starting point that helps a friend to think more deeply about the situation, talk about it, and begin to feel better.

One of the major causes of depression is someone's negative self-image—a feeling of not being smart enough, or attractive enough, or talented enough. Your friend may complain that her parents expect her to do much better in school, get into a top-rated college, or star on the school's athletic teams. Perhaps they are always comparing your friend to older siblings who seem far more successful. "Why can't they understand me and let me be myself?"

This is an opportunity for you to listen and to empathize—put yourself in someone else's shoes.

Conflicted feelings may be a natural part of adolescence, but they can also lead to anxiety and depression. As the ground shifts from under you, it may lead to confusion, uncertainty, and all kinds of internal conflicts. Who you were no longer seems comfortable. Who you are is hard to figure out much of the time. And where you're going or who you want to be may remain a total mystery.

These are often accompanied by external conflicts with your parents whose image of you may be totally different

YOUR FRIEND'S PROFILE

Before a doctor can help a new patient, the physician gathers information to create a profile. This includes past medical history, age, weight, information about the patient's parents, and symptoms of the patient's illness. A similar approach might help you in helping a friend deal with depression. Ask yourself a series of questions.

1. What are your friend's interests? How have these changed since he/she became depressed?
2. Was your friend someone who had a large group of acquaintances? Or was he/she more of a loner? Has this situation changed recently?
3. How would you describe your friend's performance in school? Was there one subject that seemed more interesting to him/her? Has this changed recently?
4. Did your friend participate in sports? Has this interest declined in recent weeks?
5. What extracurricular activities, if any, did your friend enjoy? Does he/she still enjoy them?
6. Was your friend involved in any volunteer activities? Does he/she still participate in them?
7. What hobbies did your friend enjoy? Does he/she still engage in these hobbies?
8. What activities did you and your friend participate in? Are you still doing them together or has your friend stopped?

9. Is your friend a generally optimistic or pessimistic person? Does he/she usually expect good things to happen or bad things?
10. Is your friend easily hurt if someone else criticizes him/her? How does your friend usually react?
11. Does your friend seem to dwell on and obsess about past failures or mistakes? Can he/she leave these experiences behind and move forward?
12. What do you know about your friend's family? Have there been any changes or conflicts that might have affected him/her?
13. Does your friend use drugs or drink large amounts of alcohol? If not, has this situation changed recently?
14. Is your friend looking forward to school vacation or summer vacation? If not, what seems to be the problem?
15. Has your friend mentioned anything about "not wanting to go on" or "not wanting to deal with his/her problems any longer"?
16. Have you noticed any evidence that your friend is cutting or using other forms of self-mutilation?
17. Has your friend lost a lot of weight recently and begun wearing different clothing?
18. Has your friend started missing school regularly and stopped doing homework?
19. How would you describe your friend's overall attitude toward his/her current situation?
20. Are there any other changes that you have noticed recently?

from your image of yourself. There may also be conflicts with friends, leaving you feeling isolated and rejected.

To a lesser or greater degree, these experiences are part of life for most young people. It's just that for some they seem to be more severe and gut-wrenching. While you may be fortunate enough to escape the severe form of these experiences—those that lead to major depression—it's easy to empathize with a friend who is going through them, put yourself in his place, and offer your help.

CHAPTER FIVE

GUIDING SOMEONE TOWARD A NEW CENTER

War...suicide bombings...devastating earthquakes...unchecked drought...destructive tornadoes...massive hurricanes and floods...crippling economic disasters—if you follow the news regularly, it's easy to believe that the world is a depressing place. Of course, that's only one way of looking at events—the way that the news media wants you to see things.

The media are filled with news that is negative and worrisome, which may trigger anxiety and depression.

At the same time, millions of people awake every morning, go about their work, and come home every night—many of them leading satisfying lives. So, is the glass half empty or half full? It may depend on your point of view. While some events or experiences, by their very nature, are tragic and upsetting, others become that way because of the way we see them. And this may depend on what has happened to us in the past or what we fear may occur in the future.

Ricky dreads large social events. He is shy, and any activity that requires him to talk with a group of other people makes him feel uncomfortable. At one of these events, where Ricky didn't know anyone, he almost passed out, and his girlfriend, Amy, had to help him outside. As a result, whenever a social event looms in the future and his girlfriend wants to go, Ricky becomes anxious and depressed. He anticipates that the worst will happen, he's certain that he won't have a good time, and he resists any pleas from Amy to "look on the bright side" and try to enjoy himself.

Now it's April, and the junior prom is only a couple of months away. Ricky has begun to worry about whether he will need to disappoint Amy and stay away. Even worse, she may decide to go with someone else. Nevertheless, Ricky decides not to go to the junior prom. He is also spending less and less time with friends who used to be his close pals.

"What's going on?" one of them texts him. But Ricky has no response. Every day, when school ends, he simply heads home and sits down in front of his computer screen.

His major social interactions occur over the internet instead of in person. The more time Ricky spends alone, the more he wants to stay alone.

And eventually he feels an overwhelming sense of loneliness and depression.

Ricky's story is not unusual. Feelings of isolation and depression can increase gradually until they become a way of life. It's the classic "boiling frog syndrome." A frog is placed in warm water that gradually becomes hotter and

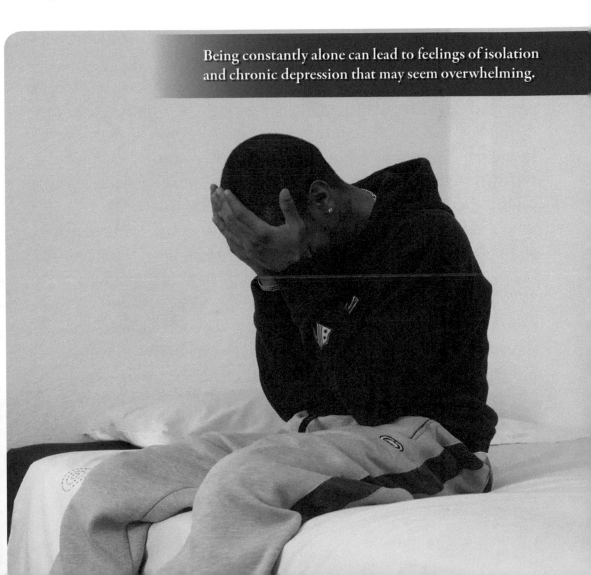

Being constantly alone can lead to feelings of isolation and chronic depression that may seem overwhelming.

hotter until, too late, the frog finds itself in a very danger-ous situation.

If you were Ricky's friend, what could you do to help him? Perhaps the best place to start is just to let him know, or show him, that you care. This may puncture the isolation bubble that your friend has built. As social worker Lisa M. Schab points out, if you ask what's causing the problem, don't be surprised if your friend answers "I don't know."

Sometimes it's not important to find the cause or trigger event. It's sufficient just to help a friend understand what's currently going on. In this case, a person's isolation may be feeding upon itself in a vicious cycle, making the feelings of depression grow worse and worse.

But as Schab points out, "The way people think directly affects their moods. One way to combat feelings of depression is by practicing positive thinking instead of negative thinking. Situations are not negative or positive within themselves. It is the thoughts we choose to think about them that make us feel happy or depressed."

An old cliché, "It's mind over matter," sometimes proves to be true. Social situations are not inherently negative. It's how we think about them that make them feel that way.

But thinking positively, especially if you've had negative experiences in the past, may be very difficult, particularly if you're feeling chronically depressed. However, you can help a friend take the first step—putting her toe in the water without necessarily taking a swim in the ocean. A re-entry into the social world with just a friend or two may be enough to begin breaking a negative pattern and puncturing the black cloud of depression.

LEAVING PAST FAILURES BEHIND

The twenty-first century has become the age of multitasking. Many of us don't focus on one thing at a time, but rather on two or three or even more things at one time. Yet studies have shown that the brain is really not very good at multitasking. Multitasking tends to undermine our ability to do things well, interfere with the ability to focus, and leave of us with the illusion of accomplishing more when we're really accomplishing less.

In a similar way, the brain is often strung between negative feelings from the past and fears about the future. Depression is often triggered by past events that keep replaying themselves over and over again. These may act like a giant ball and chain holding us back from doing things.

As a result, the future becomes a fearful place, filled with anxiety and the anticipation of bad things happening. Instead of seeing "every cloud with a silver lining," it's easy to see the reverse, with "every silver lining surrounded by a dark cloud." It's easy to watch a friend become a slave to past events and future fears, leaving him in a state of inertia that grows worse and worse, feeding the feelings of depression.

Remember that a baseball player with a .300 batting average is considered an outstanding hitter. This means that the player gets a hit only 30 percent of the time. Players will get an out seven out of the ten times that they come to the plate. If they continue to think about these outs and let the fear control their play, then it will be harder and harder to get a hit.

The great New York Yankee catcher Yogi Berra cautioned hitters not to think too much. They should just get up to the plate and focus on the ball. In other words, they need to be completely in the present—not the past or the future. And they can't let past disappointments get in the way of the immediate situation.

Some people seem to become obsessed with past failures, so much so that it paralyzes them. One of the best things that you can do for a friend who seems paralyzed by depression is to help her put past events behind her. "Putting life circumstances into a broader perspective can help...withstand disappointments and maintain a positive mood," writes Lisa Schab.

BREATHING EXERCISES

Proper breathing is often essential to a more satisfying life. Depressed or anxious people frequently take short breaths that don't bring enough oxygen into their systems. You can help someone who is feeling depressed by demonstrating simple breathing exercises.

1. Find a comfortable place to sit quietly.
2. Inhale with a deep breath through your nose.
3. Let that breath remain inside for a couple of seconds.
4. Exhale slowly through your mouth.
5. Repeat these steps until you begin to feel better.

LEARN TO MEDITATE

This is a noisy world, filled with distractions. It's quite common to see people out walking on a beautiful spring day busy talking on their cell phones or texting rather than just enjoying the experience of being outside. The present moment is forgotten as people focus on getting things done or planning for the future.

Meditation helps us to restore the balance in our lives. If you want to help a friend caught in the throes of anxiety and depression, suggest that he begin to practice the simple art of meditation. It can really help.

Meditation and deep breathing exercises can help you learn to be in the moment and enjoy the present, without being caught up in the events of the past or fears about the future.

- Find a quiet, comfortable place to sit or lie down.
- Close your eyes and begin breathing a bit more deeply.
- Try to listen to your breathing.
- You can also repeat a simple word to yourself, over and over again.
- Try to let your thoughts and worries disappear, like flowing water.
- If these thoughts intrude, don't criticize yourself, just let them flow away.
- Return to your meditation.

At first this process may be difficult. But as time goes on, it will become easier and easier. And meditation will enable you to enhance your enjoyment of the moment.

CHAPTER SIX

HELPING A FRIEND BECOME RECONNECTED

In her book *Monochrome Days: A Firsthand Account of One Teenager's Experience with Depression*, Cait Irwin wrote: "The beeping of the alarm clock sounded distant in my half-awake dream…A dark, brooding cloud was slowly casting a shadow across my mind. While I had never been an early riser, this felt different from simply being tired after staying up too late the night before. I felt weighed down, oppressed by the burden of having to face a new day. I was just waking up, and I was already exhausted by the

People need to feel connected and to enjoy a sense of community. Being alone and isolated may only increase feelings of depression.

idea of what lay ahead. The mind-cloud was starting to cast my reality in a different light."

People who are depressed feel exhausted most of the time. If you ask a friend to go out with you and spend time together, her answer is likely to be, "I can't, I'm too tired." Unfortunately, the more time a depressed person spends alone doing nothing, the more depressed she becomes. It's an unending cycle.

One of the most helpful things you can do for someone who is depressed is to help her reconnect with the outside world. This means reentering society, even if it's only one small step at a time. And you can be the person who helps your friend return.

The process of reconnecting may begin by just taking a walk together, saying nothing to your friend unless she wants to talk. Experiencing fresh air and sunshine together can help her tremendously. Simply letting a friend know you care enough to spend time with her can be reassuring and give a necessary reality check with the real world outside.

EXERCISING

Physical exercise can also be very helpful in dealing with depression—whether it's walking, jogging, swimming, gymnastics, or some other physical activity. As author Lisa Schab explains, "Physical exercise has the ability to improve mood and reduce feelings of depression. When people exercise, there is an increase in the production of the brain chemicals that lift their moods. Incorporating mild-to-moderate exercise in your daily life can help you feel less depressed."

Physical exercise is a very effective way to lift your mood and overcome feelings of depression.

Gradually, you may be able to bring your friend back in touch with one or two other people at school, in the neighborhood, or in town. Your friend may begin to join both of you in whatever you're doing together. A few caring people can make all the difference in helping someone begin the long climb out of depression.

Eventually, the circle may grow a little wider, involving other people. Humans are social animals, and isolation denies them of one of their most important needs. Social interaction also takes each of us outside ourselves. Constantly focusing on yourself only makes depression seem worse, increasing negative thoughts and anxiety about the future. Listening to other people and becoming involved in their lives gives someone with depression far less time to think about her own dark thoughts.

KEEPING A JOURNAL

Writing in a journal about your own experience with depression can be one effective way to cope with it. Writing can help a depressed person bring the inner turmoil out, look at it from a different perspective, and evaluate it. A journal can also help chart the ups and downs of a person's course through the dark tunnel of depression and hopefully out the other side. That journal should include any personal interactions that occur during this period—whether negative or positive. This will help a person determine which interactions are most influential and most positive.

VOLUNTEERING

Volunteer work, after school or on weekends, is another way to climb out of depression—especially if the activity involves working with other people. If you are involved in an after-school community project, try to persuade your friend to become involved with you. Doing something, especially with other people, is far more effective than constantly thinking and brooding by yourself.

These activities may include:
- Volunteering at a local hospital

Volunteer work, especially with other people, gives us a sense of accomplishment, of helping others, and of reconnecting with the community.

- Visiting people at a convalescent home
- Coaching a children's athletic team
- Working at a local museum
- Serving meals at a homeless shelter
- Participating in a political campaign
- Giving tours of a historical site or nature preserve
- Tutoring younger children in school

By doing something valuable, something that helps other people, an individual may also discover something he or she really enjoys. Some activities may not be appealing, but just one project can light the spark that kindles an entirely new passion and helps turn around a person's life.

CHAPTER SEVEN

SUGGESTING PROFESSIONAL HELP

As the friend of someone suffering from depression, you probably realize how difficult it can be to climb out of this situation alone. A depressed person needs to interact with others, change his mind-set, and find a new center in his personal life. The same person may also need the help of a professional counselor to deal with the problems surrounding depression and get to the root of its causes.

You might suggest that your friend seek help from an adult in school—perhaps a teacher who seems empathetic to the problems teenagers face. A school guidance counselor or school psychologist might also be helpful.

In addition, support groups might be available in your community or online. Support groups are especially useful because they enable young people suffering from depression to share their experiences with others in a similar situation. This reinforces the fact that no one needs to feel alone or feel like the only one suffering from a particular problem.

SEEKING PSYCHOLOGICAL COUNSELING

Dr. Miriam Kaufman, who has worked with teenagers for many years, has written that "depression can be treated and

Support groups provide a community where teenagers suffering from depression and anxiety can share their feelings and help each other recover.

it should be treated." She suggests that a teenager first talk to a medical doctor to ensure that some physical problem is not causing the feelings of depression. A general practitioner may also be able to recommend a psychologist or psychiatrist who is skilled at treating young people.

"Therapists use a number of tools in their work," Dr. Kaufman adds. "The most important ones are listening and observing." She cautions that anyone suffering from depression not select just any therapist, but one who specializes in helping teens with this problem. This may take some searching and some conversation with friends at school. While a good therapist will be extremely helpful, the wrong therapist may be no help at all.

CAN PARENTS HELP?

Sometimes parents can be very helpful to a son or daughter trying to cope with depression—especially if the parent is likely to understand the situation. Parents can provide important perspectives from their own lives and even share similar situations that they confronted years earlier. But not all parents fall into this category. Some react negatively to a teenager's psychological problems or brush the issues aside as a product of their son's or daughter's imagination. Their advice might be stop complaining, or "just snap out of it," without ever trying to understand the causes behind the depression. You and your friend should therefore tread softly and slowly before involving parents in this type of problem.

Therapy can take place in a setting where the therapist works one on one with a patient. The therapy sessions may continue for several weeks or months, and the therapist may even suggest antidepressant medication to assist in treatment. Therapy may also take place in a group setting with other teenagers. This is usually far less expensive and may have the added advantage of breaking down a teenager's feelings of isolation.

Major depression is a problem that occurs with many teenagers. But as a friend of someone with depression, you

A therapist who specializes in helping teens can prove invaluable in providing insights and suggesting coping mechanisms for dealing successfully with depression.

can help. Listening and empathizing can be extremely valuable in providing support and breaking down loneliness and isolation.

Suggestions for self-help can be valuable as well—helping a friend recenter himself or herself around positive thoughts rather than negative ones and becoming reconnected to the community. Finally, you can emphasize that professional help is nothing to be ashamed of but may, indeed, offer the best opportunity of success in overcoming depression.

MYTHS AND FACTS

MYTH: A psychological problem is a sign of weakness.

FACT: A problem like major depression is just as serious as a broken leg or some other physical problem. It generally needs treatment by a doctor, just like a broken bone.

MYTH: The best thing you can do with a psychological problem is "suck it up and deal with it."

FACT: This is often the worst approach you can take. It is better to seek help from a friend, counselor, parent, teacher, or psychologist.

MYTH: A serious psychological problem like major depression should make you feel ashamed.

FACT: Millions of people, many of them teenagers, suffer from this type of problem. And a large number of them admit the problem and seek help.

GLOSSARY

ANOREXIA An unrealistic body image driving someone to eat very little.

ANXIETY A general feeling of unease and fear of the future.

BULIMIA Regular purging after eating in order to stay thin.

CLINICAL DEPRESSION A major, long-term depression.

DEPRESSANT A drug that lowers brain activity.

DEPRESSION A psychological illness; a mood disorder.

DOPAMINE A chemical neurotransmitter.

DUAL DIAGNOSIS Having two illnesses, such as depression and anxiety.

ENDORPHIN Chemical released by the brain providing a feeling of well-being.

GENERAL ANXIETY DISORDER An uncontrollable feeling that something unpleasant is going to happen.

KUTCHER ADOLESCENT DEPRESSION SCALE A method of evaluating serious depression.

MELANCHOLIA An early description of depression.

NEUROTRANSMITTER A chemical that speeds messages from the brain.

NOREPINEPHRINE A chemical type of neurotransmitter.

OBSESSIVE-COMPULSIVE DISORDER Repetitive behavior with no basis in reality.

PANIC DISORDER Excessive anxiety and panic attacks.

REACTIVE DEPRESSION Depression that begins in reaction to an event.

SELF-MUTILATION Self-harming behavior such as cutting yourself.

SEROTONIN A hormone in the brain, essential for sending signals.

SOCIAL PHOBIA Fear of social situations.

TRIGGER EVENT An event that may lead to depression.

FOR MORE INFORMATION

American Psychiatric Association
1000 Wilson Boulevard
Arlington, VA 22209
(888) 357-7924
Website: http://www.psych.org
With more than forty thousand members, the American
   Psychiatric Association offers help to those suffering from
   depression and other psychological illnesses.

Canadian Mental Health Association
1110 Slater Street
Ottawa, ON KIP 5H3
Canada
(613) 745-7750
Website: http://www.cmha.ca/about-cmha
This association offers crisis lines and information to deal with
   mental health problems in children and adults.

International Foundation for Research and Education on
   Depression
PO Box 17598
Baltimore, MD 21297
(410) 268-0044
Website: http://www.ifred.org
This foundation informs the general public about the causes
   and treatment of depression.

Mental Health America
2200 N. Beauregard Street
Alexandria, VA 22311

(800) 969-6642
Website: http://www.mentalhealthamerica.net
An organization that provides the latest, most up-to-date advice
  about how to deal with psychological problems, including
  depression.

Mood Disorders of Ontario
36 Eglinton Avenue
Toronto, ON M4R 1A1
Canada
(888) 486-8236
Website: http://www.mooddisorders.ca/faq
This group provides answers to frequently asked questions
  about depression and other psychological disorders.

National Alliance for the Mentally Ill
3803 N. Fairfax Drive
Arlington, VA 22203
(703) 524-7600
Website: http://www.nami.org
The organization offers help to friends and families of those
  with psychological problems.

National Mental Health Association
2000 N. Beauregard Street
Alexandria, VA 22311
(703) 684-7722
Website: http://www.nmha.org
This association offers information on various types of mental
  illness, such as anxiety and depression.

National Mental Health Information Center
6001 Executive Boulevard, MSC 9663

Bethesda, MD 20892
(866) 615-6464
Website: http://www.nimh.nih.gov
This government agency provides help for those suffering from
  mental health problems, including anxiety, eating disorders,
  and depression.

WEBSITES

Because of the changing nature of internet links, Rosen Publishing has developed an online list of websites related to the
subject of this book. This site is updated regularly. Please use
this link to access this list:

http://www.rosenlinks.com/HCIH/depress

FOR FURTHER READING

Davis, Denise. *Teenage Depression: How to Recognize the Signs.* Amazon Digital Services, 2015.

Foster, Patrice. *A Guide for Teenage Depression.* Amazon Digital Services, 2015.

Letran, Jacqui. *I Would, but My Damn Mind Won't Let Me.* New York, NY: A Healed Mind, 2015.

McDonah, Thomas, and Jon Patrick Hatcher. *101 Ways to Conquer Teen Anxiety: Simple Tips, Techniques, and Strategies for Overcoming Anxiety, Worry and Panic.* Berkeley, CA: Ulysses Press, 2016.

Perlman, Deborah. *A Parent's Guide for Recognizing the Signs of Teenage Depression and Helping Your Child Find Happiness Again.* Amazon Digital Services, 2015.

Ross, Michele. *Signs of Depression in Teens.* Amazon Digital Services, 2014.

Saltzman, Amy, MD. *A Still Quiet Place for Teens: A Mindfulness Workbook.* Oakland, CA: Instant Help Books, 2016.

Schab, Lisa M. *Beyond the Blues: A Workbook to Help Teens Overcome Depression.* Oakland, CA: Instant Help Books, 2008.

Schwartz, Tina. *Depression: The Ultimate Teen Guide.* London, UK: Rowman and Littlefield, 2014.

Van Dijk, Sheri. *Don't Let Your Emotions Run Your Life for Teens.* Oakland, CA: Instant Help Books, 2011.

BIBLIOGRAPHY

Berlinger, Norman. *Rescuing Your Teenager from Depression.* New York, NY: Harper and Row, 2005.

Cobain, Beverly. *When Nothing Matters Anymore: A Survival Guide for Depressed Teens.* Minneapolis, MN: Free Spirit Publishing, 1998.

Irwin, Cait. *Monochrome Days: A Firsthand Account of One Teenager's Experience with Depression.* New York, NY: Oxford University Press, 2007.

Kaufman, Miriam. *Overcoming Teen Depression: A Guide for Parents.* Buffalo, NY: Firefly Books, 2001.

Psychology Tools. "Kutcher Adolescent Depression Scale." 2016. https://psychology-tools.com/kutcher-adolescent -depression-scale.

Sales, Nancy Jo. *American Girls: Social Media and the Secret Lives of Teenagers.* New York, NY: Knopf, 2016.

Scowen, Kate. *My Kind of Sad: What It's Like to Be Young and Depressed.* Toronto, ON: Annick Press, 2007.

INDEX

A

alcohol/alcohol abuse, 23–24
American Girls: Social Media and the Secret Lives of Teenagers, 10
anorexia, 27–28
antidepressant medication, 6, 52
anxiety, 9–10, 16–20, 25, 30, 31, 33, 41, 42, 43, 47

B

breathing exercises, 42
bulimia, 27–28

C

counseling/therapy, 50–53
cutting/self-mutilation, 24–26

D

depression/major depression
and anxiety, 10, 19–20
causes of, 9, 10, 11–13, 33
and genetic history, 6, 9
professional help for, 50–53
statistics on, 6
symptoms of, 13–14
talking to someone about, 30–31
Diana, Princess, 4
drugs/drug abuse, 23–24
dual diagnosis, 24, 28

E

eating disorders, 27–28
exercise, 46–47

F

Freud, Sigmund, 6

G

generalized anxiety disorder (GAD), 16, 17

H

Hippocrates, 4–6

I

inner turmoil, 11
Irwin, Cait, 45–46

ABOUT THE AUTHOR

Richard Worth is an award-winning writer who has written books for young adults on history, biography, current events, foreign affairs, science, art, self-help, and family living.

PHOTO CREDITS

Cover Monkey Business Images/Shutterstock.com; p. 5 Bettman/Getty Images; p. 9 Doug Martin/Science Source/Getty Images; p. 12 Sebastian Kaulitzki/Shutterstock.com; p. 15 Eric O'Connell/The Image Bank/Getty Images; p. 19, 32 BSIP/UIG/Universal Images Group/Getty Images; p. 22 Brasil2/E+/Getty Images; p. 25 JOTI/Science Photo Library/Getty Images; p. 27 PeopleImages/DigitalVision/Getty Images; p. 29 Alex Potemkin/E+/Getty Images; p. 37 AFP Photo/Getty Images; p. 39 Lihee Avidan/Photonica World/Getty Images; p. 43 Chris Clinton/The Image Bank/Getty Images; p. 45 Tetra Images/Getty Images; p. 47 Adam Hester/DigitalVision/Getty Images; p. 49 Hero Images/Getty Images; p. 51 Steve Debenport/E+/Getty Images; p. 53 © iStockphoto.com/sturti; cover and interior pages background images © iStockphoto.com/chaluk.

Designer: Brian Garvey; Photo Researcher: Nicole Baker; Editor: Lydia Gay